A SIMPLE GUIDE TO PRAYER

Batool Al-Toma

A Presentation by

THE ISLAMIC FOUNDATION

A Simple Guide to Prayer for Beginners

A Presentation by

The Islamic Foundation

Quran House, P.O. Box 30611, Nairobi, Kenya

P.M.B. 3193, Kano, Nigeria

Fifth impression, 2015/1436 H

Distributed by

KUBE PUBLISHING LTD.

Markfield Conference Centre

Ratby Lane, Markfield,

Leicestershire, LE67 9SY

United Kingdom

Tel: +44 (0) 1530 249230

Fax: +44 (0) 1530 249656

Email: info@kubepublishing.com

Website: www.kubepublishing.com

ISBN 978-0-86037-486-2

Cover design by Nasir Cadir

Cover photo by Batool Al-Toma

Book design & typeset by Imtiaze Ahmed Manjra

Printed by Imak Ofset, Turkey

Contents

Chapter III

Chapter IV

Chapter V

Chapter VI

Chapter VII

Appendix

Preface

Praise be to Allah, you have chosen Islam to be your way of life. Now you would naturally like to start learning and practising Islam in your daily life, as much as you can. The first and most important step on this path is that you start performing Prayers.

This book, accompanied by a CD and Pocket Guide, has been prepared for just that purpose: to support you as you embark on this process of learning and performing Prayers. They have been compiled from the very important Islamic viewpoint: that nothing that Islam requires you to learn or practise is difficult. Indeed everything should facilitate the fulfilment of your daily life, enhancing its value and joy, rather than become an obstacle or a burden for you. They have been compiled also with mindful consideration of the experiences expressed by those who, on embarking on their chosen journey into Islam, have found some of the available literature particularly confusing and overburdening at this important transitional stage.

These guidelines, we hope, will assist you towards understanding the meaning of Prayer, its form and significance as well as learning how to perform it. Once you have accepted and declared your faith – Islam – your concern must be to purify and develop both your heart and your behaviour. This is a continuous and life-long process. It is achieved by making everything you do in life an act of worship: eating, drinking, the physical relationship with your spouse, earning a livelihood, friendships. It is easy. You do everything for the sake of Allah alone, avoiding those things which He dislikes, things which you would naturally be ashamed of. Prayers help you to make your everyday life a life of worship, without disturbing your normal activities.

While we hope that this provision will be a great help, it is important for you to seek out regular contacts during which learning opportunities will present themselves as you come to know and interact more with the Muslims in your area. Attending the congregational Prayers in the local Mosque should be highly useful for this purpose. By watching, listening and joining in, you can enjoy the blessings of communal worship as well as develop your skills and confidence. Never be deterred when you feel the need to ask 'How, when, where or why?'; sincere Muslims will value your questions and be thankful for an opportunity to help. To learn is a virtue as much as it is an aid towards self development.

As you perhaps know by now, Muslims are required to learn and recite their Prayers in Arabic, and according to a given sequence. Though at first glance it may look substantial, in reality the extent of what has to be remembered is little, as there is considerable repetition throughout the Prayer. To Pray in Arabic is not only to use the language through which Allah has communicated with us, but it also brings with it a unifying dimension as Muslims throughout the world Pray in exactly the same manner and in the same language.

Some of the most important factors are highlighted here: the main purpose of the Prayer is to take you away, for a few moments, from your routine activities, to remember Allah and spend some time in your Lord's presence. To be conscious of this fact, together with millions of other Muslims, is sufficient for you to acquire the spiritual blessings of the Prayer.

That you understand both what you are saying and what you are doing is most important. Therefore:

(i) Start with the essentials.
(ii) Keep them simple and correct.
(iii) Learn a little more, regularly, if possible.

The New Muslims Project would like to express sincere thanks and heartfelt gratitude to all those who took the time to read the manuscript, offered suggestions for its improvement and helped bring it to its final stage of publication. We are especially grateful to Sheikh Abdullah Al-Judai, Director of the Islamic Research Centre, Leeds who, in his capacity as member of the European Council for Fatwa and Research, read the manuscript and advised on matters of *Fiqh*. A special note of thanks for his gentle advice in this, and his unrelenting support for the New Muslims Project generally, must go to our dear departed Br. Khurram Murad who would wish only that you remember him in your Prayers.

Batool Al-Toma
New Muslims Project
The Islamic Foundation

CHAPTER ONE

Introduction to Prayer in Islam

ṢALĀH

Ṣalāh or Prayer is the second of the five pillars of Islam after *Shahāda* – to testify to the oneness of Allah and the Prophethood of Muḥammad (PBUH). The other three are: *Zakāh* – an obligatory charge on your wealth paid annually for those in need; *Ṣawm* – fasting during the month of *Ramaḍan*, and *Ḥajj* – making the pilgrimage to Makka (if it is within your means). However, just as a building does not consist only of four walls, Islam does not exist on these five pillars alone but is a complete way of life encompassing all aspects of the spiritual, moral and physical well-being of humankind.

The first pillar – *Shahāda*, that is to testify that there is no god but Allah and that Muḥammad (PBUH) is His Messenger – is the pivot around which the whole of Islam revolves. The second – mandatory daily Prayers – is the most direct way of communicating with Allah, of establishing and nourishing that personal relationship with your Lord and Sustainer, without which you cannot be a good Muslim.

Prayer is the most direct way of communicating with Allah, of establishing and nourishing that personal relationship with your Lord and Sustainer

The Arabic word *Ṣalāh* is a wide and comprehensive term which cannot be adequately translated by the English term 'Prayer'. *Ṣalāh*, while it embodies the concepts of supplication, petition and invocation implied in the English term 'Prayer', is much more than this.

Prayer in Islam is not merely a series of words and movements practised occasionally, or even regularly, without much thought as to its meaning or purpose. Rather it is a comprehensive form of communication with Allah which, if it is 'established' in the heart, brings the desired results and ties the individual and the community to their Lord in a fruitful and positive way. It awakens your heart to your Lord and becomes the practical expression of your love for your Creator. Withdrawing from the mundane matters of life, and turning towards Allah, knowing that He is not only listening but responding to each worshipper, creates a warm, cherished feeling within, knowing that the love shown to your Creator is reciprocated seven hundred-fold.

Turning towards Allah, knowing that He is not only listening but responding to each worshipper, creates a warm, cherished feeling within, knowing that the love shown to your Creator is reciprocated seven hundred-fold

There are no shows of extravagance connected to the performance of Prayer. It is a simple and humbling exercise prior to which you are requested to observe some basic aspects of cleanliness and purity, referred to as ablution or *Wuḍū*. The Prayer, once it is truly understood, gives an infinite strength to live by the will of Allah, to abstain from what He dislikes and to deal with the trials of life with commitment and confidence in Him. It can be the best consolation and means of encouragement during times of stress and anxiety.

The Qur'ān continuously encourages the observance of Prayer:

And be steadfast in Prayer and give in charity; and whatever good you send ahead of you for your souls you shall find it with Allah: for Allah sees all that you do.
(*Sūrah* 2: 110)

Guard strictly your Prayers, especially the middle Prayer, and stand before Allah in a devout manner.
(*Sūrah* 2: 238)

Great importance is attached to the conscious observance of the Prayer as it is the first thing about which you will be questioned and held accountable for on the Day of Judgement.

There is abundant evidence in the Qur'ān that Prayer was a requirement and was practised in some form or another by the earlier Prophets and their followers, as an essential part of their relationship with Allah. Prophet Abraham (PBUH) sought Allah's grace and support in his efforts to establish Prayer among his people:

My Lord, make me establish regular Prayer, and make my offspring do likewise, my Lord, accept my supplication.
(*Sūrah* 14: 40)

Allah spoke to Prophet Moses (PBUH), saying:

Verily I am Allah, there is no god but I, so serve Me only and perform Prayer for the remembrance of Me.
(*Sūrah* 20: 14)

Prayer is the first thing about which you will be questioned and held accountable for on the Day of Judgement

Prophet Jesus (PBUH) said of his Lord:

And He made me blessed wherever I may be, and He enjoined upon me Prayer and Almsgiving as long as I live.
(*Sūrah* 19: 31)

In the same way the instruction to pray was reaffirmed in the Qur'ān to become the cornerstone of the mission of Prophet Muḥammad (PBUH).

And recite, (O Prophet), what is sent of the Book to you, and perform regular Prayer: for Prayer restrains from shameful and evil deeds; and remembrance of Allah is the greatest thing in life without doubt. And Allah knows the deeds that you do.
(*Sūrah* 29: 45)

Prayer, therefore, is a key to several different treasures. It is a means of remembering Allah, our Creator and the Source of everything which surrounds us; it is a means through which we seek His help and guidance so that our lives will be more fruitful here and in the Hereafter, as we strive to live according to His will; it is a time to ask for forgiveness from Allah for our faults and to sincerely thank Him for the treasures He has provided us with and for the bounties we have received, both material and spiritual.

Prayer is a means of remembering Allah and seeking His help and guidance to strive to live according to His will

New Beginnings

You have just recited your *Shahāda* – testifying to the Oneness of Allah and the Prophethood of Muḥammad (PBUH) thereby entering the fold of Islam. It is now necessary that you perform *Ghusl* – take a full shower.

This is an act of purification which you should attend to as soon as the opportunity presents itself.

In the meantime those other Muslims present who have just witnessed this joyous occasion are inviting you to join them for the Prayer. It is understandable that you may not be familiar with the Prayer and its requirements at this stage and therefore feel a little apprehensive – however, this is an important learning experience the observance of which should not be missed.

Since this is a communal Prayer, the *Imām*, by leading it, takes on the responsibility of the Prayer for the rest of the worshippers. The worshipers should not make any movement ahead of the *Imām*, nor should they anticipate any of his movements but together, as a unified congregation, they follow his movements which are (with one exception) preceded by the words *Allāhu Akbar* – 'Allah is Greatest' – until the final *Salām* to his right and then left shoulder which concludes the Prayer.

For some time, when the time for the Prayer arrives, because you are new to Islam you may find yourself in the same predicament. Prepare yourself for Prayer by first performing ablution – *Wuḍū'*. Then simply follow the movement procedure of the Prayer. You may remember and praise Allah by using simple phrases which you find easy to recall such as *Allāhu Akbar* – 'Allah is Greatest', *Subḥān Allāh* – 'Glory to Allah', *Al-Ḥamdulillāh* – 'All Praise is due to Allah' and complete the movement sequence to the end. You may feel the need to hold a guide to Prayer in your hand or listen to a recording of the Prayer, repeating as you hear the words. In time you will be able to memorise and recall the entire procedure.

***Ghusl* is an act of purification which you should attend to as soon as the opportunity presents itself.**

We hope that by reading on, these guidelines will help you towards achieving that goal.

The Obligatory or *Farḍ* Prayers

It is preferable that we first understand, learn and feel confident with the obligatory or *Farḍ* Prayers of which there are five. These are performed at different intervals during the day:

1. *Fajr* or Dawn Prayer – performed between the break of dawn and the approach of sunrise.

2. *Ẓuhr* or Noon Prayer – performed from just past mid-day until mid-afternoon.

3. *ʿAṣr* or Afternoon Prayer – performed from mid-afternoon to the approach of sunset.

4. *Maghrib* or Sunset Prayer – performed immediately after sunset and before darkness falls.

5. *ʿIshā'* or Night Prayer – performed from after dark until just before dawn.

Because the Prayer times relate to the earth's position to the sun, they constantly change throughout the year. They also vary according to where in the world you are living

Because the Prayer times relate to the earth's position to the sun, they constantly change throughout the year. They also vary according to where in the world you are living. These guidelines, therefore, together with the following diagram are general. For accuracy it is best to secure a Prayer time-table from a Muslim friend or a local Mosque.

This diagram, we hope, will help you to ascertain the approximate time for each Prayer.

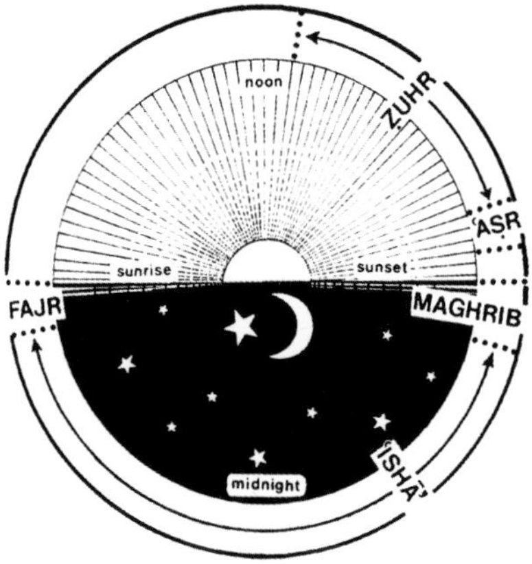

Timings of Daily Prayers

The Time to Perform Prayers

It is necessary and important that Prayers are performed within the time allowed and according to your own or the community's convenience. All Prayers are preferred to be performed at the beginning of their time except the night Prayer – *ʿIshā'*, which is preferred to be prayed at its later time or before retiring to bed. It is not desirable to delay the Prayer deliberately through neglect and apathy, which clearly reflects a person's attitude towards Allah. Try never to miss the Prayer altogether.

It is not desirable to delay the Prayer deliberately through neglect and apathy, which clearly reflects a person's attitude towards Allah. Try never to miss the Prayer altogether

The collective Prayer, in the Mosque, may be delayed in order that the maximum number of people may participate, *i.e.* in the case of the dawn Prayer during summer, or the noon Prayer during winter being delayed to the optimum lunch-time slot of one o'clock for university students or those who are working so that they may pray in their lunch break.

Where to Perform the Prayer

Performance of the Prayer requires no special place or building. The only requirement is that the area chosen should be clean and free from impurities, in the same way as the body must be free from anything regarded as impure and which would require you to renew your ablution – *Wuḍū'*. Consequently, persons who are away from their homes, travelling or working, may pray wherever they are: in a quiet, convenient or even designated area in the workplace, the park, the railway station or the airport. It is always preferable that you choose an area where you do not disturb or cannot easily be disturbed by others.

You can also pray inside a moving vehicle in the sitting position if you cannot get out of the vehicle within the allowed time for the Prayer. Similarly in the event of illness, pregnancy, disability, exhaustion or merely tiredness, you can pray sitting or lying down. If you are able, you must make symbolic gestures with the head, eyes, hand or finger comparable to that of the movement sequence in the Prayer.

Performance of the Prayer requires no special place or building. The only requirement is that the area chosen should be clean and free from impurities

The Direction of Prayer – *Qibla*

Muslims, wherever they may be, are required to face towards the Kaʿba in Makka to pray. This is an essential condition, which, if not met, makes the Prayer invalid. This direction is called *Qibla*. The Kaʿba is the first house on earth built for the worship of Allah alone. It is thus a symbol of monotheism or *Tawḥīd* in Islam and also of the unity of the mission of all the Prophets of Allah, as much as it symbolises the unity of the Muslim community.

Muslims, therefore, pray neither to the East (as is commonly misunderstood) nor to the West but to Allah alone in the direction of the *Qibla*, which every Muslim must endeavour to ascertain. For those with a good sense of direction, this can be sought through knowledge of the movement of the sun, moon and stars. It is more commonly defined, however, by the use of a compass.

From the UK the direction of the *Qibla* is South East. If you find yourself in a place where you simply do not know the direction of the *Qibla*, then choose the direction, using your best judgement, and pray leaving the rest to Allah. When Praying inside a moving vehicle in the sitting position obviously you will have to pray towards the direction you are travelling. It is best however, to partially turn your body or at least your head in the direction of the *Qibla*, if it is known to you, for part or all of the Prayer. At times like this Allah knows full well your intention as well as your difficulties and circumstances and He is all-Knowing and all-Forgiving. Keep in mind that it is always necessary to pray whatever the circumstances and, though you may be unable to face towards it or locate it, in your heart you must have this sense of direction towards the *Qibla*.

Muslims, wherever they may be, are required to face towards the Kaʿba in Makka to pray. This is an essential condition, which, if not met, makes the Prayer invalid. This direction is called *Qibla*

What to Wear

When preparing to meet someone you know and respect as a friend, or responding to an invitation to meet a dignitary or someone in a position of authority, you take care to dress properly. Similarly, when performing the Prayer before Allah, you should dress in a fitting and decent manner.

Your clothing does not have to be any different from that which you normally wear. Whatever you wear, it will be condidered acceptable by Islamic teachings, provided it is decent and respectable and that it is clean. The minimum requirement for men to be able to perform Prayer before Allah is that they should be covered from the navel to the knees. A woman's whole body should be covered for the Prayer except the face, hands and feet, which she is not required to cover.

Shoes are always removed when Prayers are performed inside so that the Prayer area remains clean. For this reason also you will notice that Muslims generally remove their shoes when entering the Mosque and their own or the homes of other Muslims.

Many items, such as Prayer mats, beads and specific garments have come to be looked upon as essential requirements for Prayer. In truth, these things have come about as part of Islamic culture and associated community traditions have developed historically. Male headgear, which was worn by the Prophet Muḥammad (PBUH) from time to time, may be worn but is not an essential requirement for Prayer. Finally, whatever you may find to put on or whatever you are wearing, you should pray rather than miss the Prayer due to improper dress, unless it is soiled with impurities.

... when performing the Prayer before Allah, you should dress in a fitting and decent manner

CHAPTER TWO

Ablution or *WUḌŪ'*

Preparing for Prayer requires making ready your body as well as your heart and mind, since all of these will participate in the Prayer. To prepare your body, you are required to wash certain parts like the face, hands and feet. This is called *Wuḍū'*. Its purpose is for you to acquire a sense of purity as you get ready to stand in the presence of your Creator Who is Absolutely Pure. The Prophet Muḥammad (PBUH) pointed out that this ablution also washes away sins committed by these organs of the body. With a sincere intention to perform the Prayer, the basic essentials of *Wuḍū'* are to wash your face and arms, wipe over your head, and wash your feet. However, a more perfect form of *Wuḍū'* which was communicated to the Prophet (PBUH) by the Angel Gabriel is outlined here: Start by saying:

The Prophet Muhammad (PBUH) pointed out that this ablution also washes away sins committed by these organs of the body

بِسْمِ اللهِ   In the name of Allah

Bismillāh

1. Wash your hands.

2. Rinse your mouth out with water.

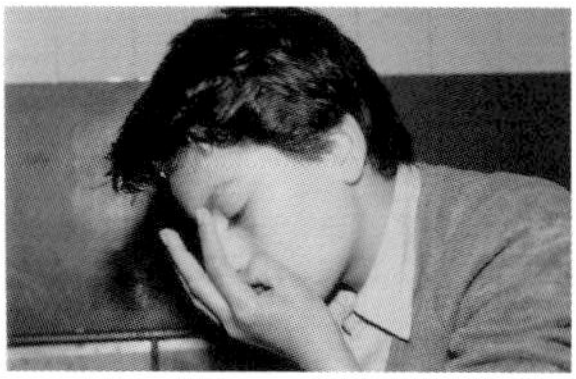

3. Clean out your nose with water.

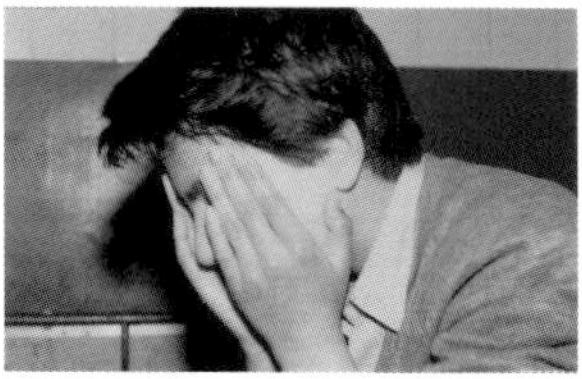

4. Wash your face.

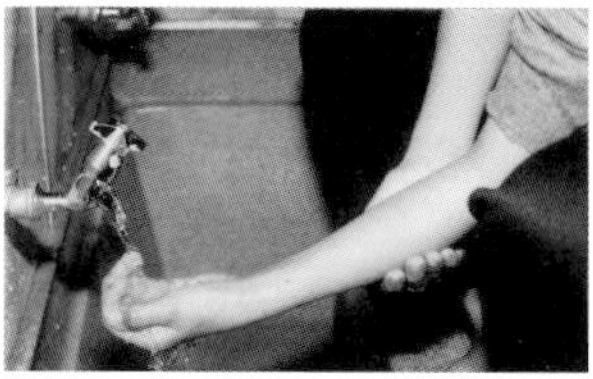

5. Wash your right and then left arm up to the elbow.

6. Pass your wet hands over your hair and wipe in and outside your ear with thumbs and index fingers.

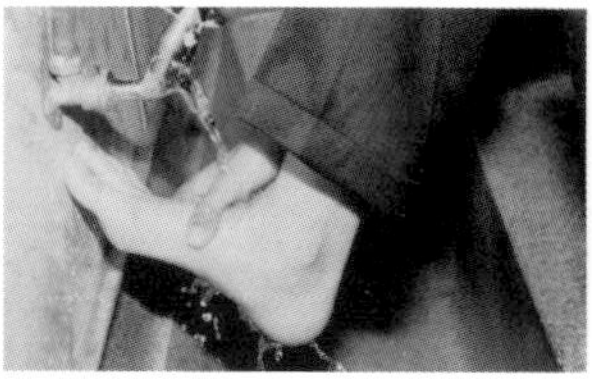

7. Wash your right and then left foot as far as the ankle.

The principle is that the washing covers the whole of these areas and that no dry patches are left. They should be washed once, twice or a recommended three times with the exception of 6 which is required just once.

Occasions Which Require *Wuḍū'* to be Repeated

It is not necessary to perform *Wuḍū'* for every Prayer if the last ablution performed is still valid. It is highly unlikely, however, that you will be able to prolong your ablution for an entire day. Things that require you to renew your ablution are:

- defecating, urinating or passing wind
- falling into a deep sleep thereby losing consciousness
- temporary loss of consciousness due to fainting spells or hysteria

Wiping Over the Socks

If you have performed *Wuḍū'*, and then put on your socks, it is not necessary to remove them every time you repeat your ablution for one day (or for three days if you are on a journey). You may wipe your wet hands over the socks to complete your *Wuḍū'* instead of washing your feet.

Occasions When a Full Shower – *Ghusl* is Required Before Prayer

You should bathe regularly so that, as an ambassador of Islam, you may present yourself and your beliefs to others in a pleasant manner. The Prophet Muḥammad (PBUH) recommended bathing at least once weekly even then, when facilities were not as they are today.

There are certain occasions however, when you are required to perform *Ghusl* – take a full shower or wash your entire body, and during which the parts of your body specified in the making of *Wuḍū'* should also be washed, before you can perform the Prayer. These occasions are:

- on entering Islam (after reciting *Shahāda*)
- after intimate relations, *i.e.* sexual intercourse between husband and wife whether semen has been ejected or not
- any discharge of semen, *i.e.* having experienced a wet dream
- when a woman has completed her monthly period*
- after childbirth when post-natal bleeding has stopped*

How to Do *Ghusl*

The aim is to wash your entire body. Begin with washing the genitals followed by the procedure for *Wuḍū'*, excluding the feet. Then wash the head and the entire body starting with the right side followed by the left and concluding with the feet. If a woman has long hair which is plaited it is not necessary for her to untie it. To throw water over it three times using her hands is sufficient, as long as water reaches the scalp.

---

* When a woman's monthly period commences she must not perform Prayer from that moment until its complete cessation. The same applies in the case of post-natal bleeding. She may only resume Prayer after performing *Ghusl* and does not have to make up for any Prayers missed during that time.

When and How to Perform Dry Ablution or *Tayammum*

There are a number of occasions when you are allowed to perform dry ablution instead of ablution with water before you perform Prayer. These are:

- Enough water to make *Wuḍū'* may not be available, *e.g.* while travelling or in the event of a drought and the time for Prayers is running out.
- You may be ill and cannot get to water or the exertion may be harmful for you.
- The use of water may be harmful, e.g. a skin condition or wounds may be aggravated by it.

If you experience any of the above or a relatively similar problematic situation you should perform dry ablution as follows:

- Strike both hands lightly on any dry, clean surface of earth.
- Wipe the face once followed by both hands to the wrists.

More about Personal Hygiene or *Ṭahārah*

Cleanliness or purity, referred to as *Ṭahārah* in the Qur'ān, indicates both spiritual and physical cleanliness, because Allah is concerned with man's moral, spiritual and material well-being. Therefore, showering and performing ablution are not the only requirements; for personal hygiene the Prophet Muḥammad (PBUH) made several recommendations. These were to pay particular attention to the teeth through use of the *Miswāk*, a naturally-grown stick with dental hygiene properties, or regular brushing with tooth-

Cleanliness or purity indicates both spiritual and physical cleanliness, because Allah is concerned with man's moral, spiritual and material well-being

brush and paste. It is also recommended that the nails should be trimmed and the pubic and underarm hair be removed or at least trimmed regularly. Washing hands before and after meals, eating properly and only from what is allowed, as well as being concerned about one's physical fitness, is also a duty on every Muslim.

Particular attention is drawn to maintaining cleanliness after having relieved yourself in the toilet. Toilet tissue can be used in the normal manner but you should also cultivate the preferred habit of cleaning yourself by carefully and thoroughly washing your private parts with water. The right hand is used for pouring while using your left hand for the washing process. This is called *Istinjā'* and can be done using a water container, a bidet or a spray hose, all of which are familiar objects in Muslim homes and Mosques throughout the UK. If water is not available, extra care should be taken to ensure cleanliness through the use of toilet tissue alone. The use of urinals for men will not allow for this procedure to work effectively therefore it is best to avoid them if possible.

Muslims are forbidden to relieve themselves in waterways or in shady areas, which should be respected for public use

Muslims are forbidden to relieve themselves in waterways or in shady areas, which should be respected for public use, and should always relieve themselves in privacy.

CHAPTER THREE

The Call to Prayer

ADHĀN AND *IQĀMA*

Adhān and *Iqāma* refer to the words called out prior to communal or *Jamā*ʿ*a* Prayer at the Mosque or indeed in any place where a group of Muslims are gathered together and will therefore pray together. For those who have only just begun to learn how to pray there is, at this stage, no necessity to learn all the words. It is, however, of value to look at and understand their meaning as they contain much of the essence and importance of the five daily Prayers.

The *Adhān* – a unique method of announcing the time for a Prayer has started, reminds everyone of the basic teachings of Islam as well as inviting him/ her to the Prayer

The *Adhān* is the call to Prayer. It has been called from the minarets or courtyards of Mosques for more than 1400 years, and always by means of the human voice. This unique method of announcing the time for a Prayer has started, reminds everyone of the basic teachings of Islam as well as inviting him/her to the Prayer. It also serves as a reminder for those living in the immediate area that they should prepare for the Prayer by making *Wuḍū'* and, for those who are able, to make their way to the Mosque, so they can Pray in congregation as desired. It is called by one of those who will take part in the Prayer or by the *Mu'adhdhin*, one who is appointed to call the *Adhān*.

The words for the *Adhān*, and the number of times they are repeated, are as follows:

اللهُ أَكْبَر *Allāhu Akbar* (4)	Allah is Greatest
أَشْهَدُ أَنْ لاَ إِلَهَ إِلاَّ الله *Ashhadu an lā ilāha illallāh* (2)	I witness that there is no god but Allah
أَشْهَدُ أَنَّ مُحَمَّداً رَسُولُ الله *Ashhadu anna Muḥammadan Rasūlullāh* (2)	I witness that Muḥammad is the Messenger of Allah
حَيَّ عَلَى الصَّلاَة *Hayya ʿalāṣ-Ṣalāh* (2)	Hurry to Prayer
حَيَّ عَلَى الْفَلاَح *Hayya ʿalāl-Falah* (2)	Hurry to success
اللهُ أَكْبَر *Allāhu Akbar* (2)	Allah is Greatest
لاَ إِلَهَ إِلاَّ الله *lā Ilāha illallāh* (1)	There is no god but Allah

The *Adhān* for the dawn, *Fajr* Prayer, differs slightly in that the following is added after *Hayya ʿalāl-Falah*:

الصَّلاَةُ خَيْرٌ مِنَ النَّوْم *Aṣṣalātu khayrun minan-nawm* (2)	Prayer is better than sleep

Just before starting the Prayer in congregation the *Iqāma* is said. The *Iqāma* serves to let those who have assembled at the place of Prayer know that an obligatory or *Farḍ* Prayer is about to begin. As it is being called those present form into neat, straight rows behind the *Imām* as he stands and prepares to lead them in Prayer.

The words of the *Iqāma* differ from those of the *Adhān* in one sentence only. The words *Qad Qāmatiṣ-Ṣalāh* are added and repeated twice to announce that the Prayer is about to commence.

The words for the *Iqāma*, and the number of times they are repeated, are as follows:

اللهُ أَكْبَر *Allāhu Akbar* (2)	Allah is Greatest
أَشْهَدُ أَنْ لاَ إِلَهَ إِلاَّ الله *Ashhadu an lā ilāha illallāh* (1)	I witness that there is no god but Allah
أَشْهَدُ أَنَّ مُحَمَّداً رَسُولُ الله *Ashhadu anna Muḥammadan Rasūlullāh* (1)	I witness that Muḥammad is the Messenger of Allah
حَيَّ عَلَى الصَّلاَة *Hayya ʿalāṣ-Ṣalāh* (1)	Hurry to Prayer
حَيَّ عَلَى الْفَلاَح *Hayya ʿalāl-Falah* (1)	Hurry to success
قَدْ قَامَتِ الصَّلاَة *Qad Qāmatiṣ-Ṣalāh* (2)	Prayer has begun

اللهُ أَكْبَر *Allāhu Akbar* (2)	Allah is Greatest
لاَ إِلَهَ إِلاَّ الله *lā Ilāha illallāh* (1)	There is no god but Allah

What is an Obligatory or *Farḍ* Prayer?

Each Prayer is composed of a number of units, each unit being called a *Rakʿa*. Some of these *Rakʿas* are performed silently or whispered to oneself. Others are audible, meaning that the verses from the Qur'ān and the words proceeding each movement are said aloud, while the rest of the Prayer is silent.

- The dawn or *Fajr* Prayer has 2 *Rakʿas* and is performed audibly
- The noon or *Ẓuhr* Prayer has 4 *Rakʿas* and is performed silently
- The afternoon or *ʿAṣr* Prayer has 4 *Rakʿas* and is performed silently
- The evening or *Maghrib* Prayer has 3 *Rakʿas*, the first two of which are performed audibly, the third silently.
- The night or *ʿIshā'* Prayer has 4 *Rakʿas*, the first two of which are performed audibly followed by two performed silently

After every two *Rakʿas* one must either finish the Prayer, as in the case of the *Fajr* Prayer which is composed only of two *Rakʿas*, or continue by resuming the standing position and repeating one or two more *Rakʿas* in order to complete one of the other four daily Prayers.

How the Prayer – *Ṣalāh,* is Performed

Prayer provides a regular opportunity to remind yourself of the Ultimate Truth; that you are here on earth only in order to live as Allah, your Creator, desires. It is a time, therefore, of contemplation and deep spiritual awakening. During it, you should not allow yourself to be distracted by disturbances which often occur around you. You should not talk, laugh, eat or drink anything or make any unnecessary or excessive motions, but concentrate, remembering that your Prayer is to and for the sake of Allah alone. Every part of you should be involved in the Prayer.

Before commencing you must be clear in your intention, *Niyya*, to perform this particular obligatory Prayer for the sake of Allah.

Standing facing the *Qibla* on clean ground, a mat or clean cover you begin by raising your hands to your ears with palms facing front, and saying:

اللهُ أَكْبَر *Allāhu Akbar*	Allah is Greatest

Then lower your arms to the centre of your body, the right hand resting on the left hand.

In this standing position the first thing you must recite is the first chapter (*Sūrah*) of the Qur'ān: *Sūrah al-Fatiḥa* or 'The Opening', the meaning of which is very beautiful:

بِسْمِ اللهِ الرَّحْمَنِ الرَّحِيمِ *Bismillāh ir-Raḥmān ir-Raḥīm*	In the name of Allah the Most Gracious the Most Merciful
ٱلْحَمْدُ لِلَّهِ رَبِّ ٱلْعَٰلَمِينَ *Al-Ḥamdu lillāhi rabbi-l-ʿĀlamīn*	All praise is due to Allah, the Lord of the worlds
ٱلرَّحْمَٰنِ ٱلرَّحِيمِ *Ar-Raḥmān ir-Raḥīm*	The Most Gracious the Most Merciful
مَٰلِكِ يَوْمِ ٱلدِّينِ *Māliki yawmid-dīn*	Master of the Day of Judgement
إِيَّاكَ نَعْبُدُ وَإِيَّاكَ نَسْتَعِينُ *Iyyāka naʿbudu wa iyyāka nastaʿīn*	You alone we worship and you alone we ask for help
ٱهْدِنَا ٱلصِّرَٰطَ ٱلْمُسْتَقِيمَ *Ihdinaṣ-ṣirāṭal-mustaqīm*	Show us the Straight way
صِرَٰطَ ٱلَّذِينَ أَنْعَمْتَ عَلَيْهِمْ *ṣirāṭal-ladhīna an ʿamta ʿalayhim*	The way of those whom You have blessed
غَيْرِ ٱلْمَغْضُوبِ عَلَيْهِمْ وَلَا ٱلضَّآلِّينَ *ghayri-l-maghḍūbi ʿalayhim walāḍ-ḍālīn*	not those who have earned your anger or gone astray.

This is followed by the word

آمين *Āmīn*	Amen

(As soon as you are able, you should recite here one other short *Sūrah* from the Qur'ān. Try to learn from the selection provided on the accompanying CD. This applies only in the first two *Rakʿas* of every Prayer.)

Having recited this *Sūrah*, you repeat the words:

اللّٰهُ أَكْبَر *Allāhu Akbar*	Allah is Greatest

and bow, with your hands gripping your knees, your back and head level. You rest in this position, called *Rukūʿ*, and repeat three times:

سُبْحَانَ رَبِّيَ الْعَظِيم *Subḥāna Rabbi al-ʿAẓīm*	Glory to Allah the Great

While returning to the upright position, you say:

سَمِعَ اللّٰهُ لِمَنْ حَمِدَه *Samiʿa Allāhu liman ḥamida*	Allah hears the one who praises Him

followed (in the upright position) by

رَبَّنَا وَلَكَ الْحَمْد *Rabanā walakal-ḥamd*	Our Lord, Praise be to you

You then repeat the words:

اللّٰهُ أَكْبَر *Allāhu Akbar*	Allah is Greatest

and prostrate yourself before Allah.

Prostration, *Sajda*, is a sign of your complete submission in all humility to Allah. From the standing position, lower yourself to a kneeling position, your forehead and nose touching the ground, the palms of your hands flat on the ground each side of your head. With your arms and elbows slightly off the floor you are now in the prostration position. While in this position you repeat three times:

سُبْحَانَ رَبِّيَ الأَعْلَى *Subḥāna Rabbi al-Aʿlā*	Glory be to my Lord, the Most High

Then say:

اللهُ أَكْبَر *Allāhu Akbar*	Allah is Greatest

and sit back on your feet for a few moments, resting your hands on your thighs near to your knees. In this position it is highly recommended to supplicate and ask Allah for Forgiveness and Mercy.

After a moment or two say:

اللهُ أَكْبَر *Allāhu Akbar*	Allah is Greatest

and return to the prostration position, using the same words as before. This brings to an end one *Rakʿa* of the Prayer.

To complete the second *Rakʿa* you repeat the words:

اللهُ أَكْبَر *Allāhu Akbar*	Allah is Greatest

and resume the original standing position, repeating the entire procedure up to this point.

To finish the Prayer you repeat the words:

اللهُ أَكْبَر *Allāhu Akbar*	Allah is Greatest

and resume the sitting position similar to that assumed between the two prostrations. Resting comfortably in that position you raise your right index finger and recite the following Prayer known as the *Tashahhud*.

التَّحِيَّاتُ لله *At-Taḥiyyātu Lillāhi*	All greetings is for Allah
وَالصَّلَوَاتُ وَالطَّيِّبَاتُ *Waṣ-Ṣalawātu Wat-Ṭayyibātu*	and Prayers and goodness
السَّلَامُ عَلَيْكَ أَيُّهَا النَّبِيُّ *As-salāmu ʿAlayka Ayyuhan-Nabiyyu*	Peace be on you, O Prophet
وَرَحْمَةُ اللهِ وَبَرَكَاتُه *Wa Raḥmatullāhi Wa Barakātuhu*	and the Mercy and Blessings of Allah
السَّلَامُ عَلَيْنَا وَعَلَى عِبَادِ اللهِ الصَّالِحِين *As-salāmu ʿAlaynā wa ʿAlā Ibādillāhiṣ-Ṣāliḥīn*	Peace be on us and on the righteous servants of Allah

أَشْهَدُ أَنْ لَا إِلَهَ إِلَّا اللهُ *Ashhadu an lā illāha illallāh*	I bear witness that there is no god but Allah
وَأَشْهَدُ أَنَّ مُحَمَّداً *Wa ashhadu anna Muḥammadan*	and I bear witness that Muḥammad
عَبْدُهُ وَرَسُولُه *ʿAbduhu wa Rasūluh*	is His servant and His messenger

This is followed by the Prayer known as *Ṣalat ʿalā al-Nabī*, 'Prayer on the Prophet (PBUH)'. (This supplication is recommended although the obligatory Prayer would not be defective without it. It is advisable therefore, to learn it as soon as you can.)

اللَّهُمَّ صَلِّ عَلَى مُحَمَّدٍ *Allāhumma ṣallī ʿalā Muḥammad*	O Allah, send Prayers on Muḥammad,
وَعَلَى آلِ مُحَمَّد *wa ʿalā āli Muḥammad*	and on the family of Muḥammad
كَمَا صَلَّيْتَ عَلَى إِبْرَاهِيمَ *kamā ṣallayta ʿalā Ibrāhīm*	as You sent Prayers on Ibrahim
وَعَلَى آلِ إِبْرَاهِيمَ *wa ʿalā ʿali Ibrāhīm*	and his family,
إِنَّكَ حَمِيدٌ مَجِيد *innaka ḥamidūn majīd*	You are indeed worthy of Praise, full of Glory.

اللّٰهُمَّ بَارِكْ عَلَى مُحَمَّدٍ *Allāhumma Bārik ʿalā Muḥammad*	O Allah, send Blessings on Muḥammad
وَعَلَى آلِ مُحَمَّد *wa ʿalā āli Muḥammad*	and on the family of Muḥammad
كَمَا بَارَكْتَ عَلَى إِبْرَاهِيمَ *kamā bārakta ʿalā Ibrāhīm*	as You blessed Ibrahim
وَعَلَى آلِ إِبْرَاهِيم *wa ʿalā āli Ibrāhīm*	and the family of Ibrahim,
إِنَّكَ حَمِيدٌ مَجِيد *innaka ḥamidūn majīd*	You indeed are worthy of Praise full of Glory.

Finally, turning your head to the right and looking towards your shoulder, say:

السَّلَامُ عَلَيْكُمْ وَرَحْمَةُ الله *As-Salāmu ʿAlaykum wa Raḥmatullāh*	The peace and Mercy of Allah be with you

and turning your head to the left and looking towards your shoulder, say:

السَّلَامُ عَلَيْكُمْ وَرَحْمَةُ الله *As-Salāmu ʿAlaykum wa Raḥmatullāh*	The peace and Mercy of Allah be with you

This *Salām* completes the actions for the dawn or *Fajr* Prayer.

If you are performing one of the other four daily Prayers which necessitates one or two more *Rakʿas*, you simply recite the *Tashahhud* after the first two *Rakʿas*, then resume the standing position repeating:

اللهُ أَكْبَرُ Allāh is Greatest
Allāhu Akbar

and complete one or two more *Rakʿas* (according to the Prayer in question) ending with the *Tashahhud* (and *as-Ṣalāt ʿalā an-Nabī* when you are able) and make the final *Salām*.

To understand this procedure more fully, see the performance of prayer with illustrations, Chapter 7, page 59 of this manual, together with the accompanying CD.

Varying Schools of Thought

Please note that there are slight variations relating to both the actions and the words used in the Prayer depending on the school of law being followed. There is no need to concern yourself should you notice some of these differences when you are Praying in congregation or if they are pointed out to you by a well-meaning person in the Mosque. As your knowledge of Islam grows and develops you will come to appreciate those slight differences more and understand that they are all acceptable in that they do not affect the validity of your Prayer.

CHAPTER FOUR

CONGREGATIONAL PRAYER AND WHEN IT MUST BE PERFORMED

Every obligatory Prayer should be performed in *Jamāʿa* – congregation, if possible. According to the Prophet Muḥammad (PBUH), Prayer in congregation brings 27 times the reward of Prayer performed individually and this recommendation applies to all Muslims.

There are a number of Prayers, however, which are Prayed only in congregation. They are:

- Friday or *Jumuʿa* Prayer.
- Prayer performed on the occasion of the two major festivals *ʿĪd al-Fiṭr* and *ʿĪd al-Aḍḥā*.
- Funeral or *Janāza* Prayer for the deceased.

The format of the Prayer performed in congregation is the same as that performed by the individual. If you are a man attending congregational Prayer you should stand next to the other men present in straight, complete rows behind the *Imām*. You should not make a movement ahead of the

... Prayer in congregation brings 27 times the reward of Prayer performed individually and this recommendation applies to all Muslims

Imām nor should you anticipate his movements but, together with the entire congregation, follow his movements which are signalled by the words *Allāhu Akbar*, 'Allah is Greatest'. He brings the Prayer to a conclusion by making the *Salām* towards his right and then left shoulder.

Women also pray in congregation, either by joining together with the family, neighbourhood or at community level by attending congregational Prayers at the Mosque, where they may pray in rows behind the men or in a separate area provided for them elsewhere in the Mosque.

When a group of women pray in congregation where one of them acts as the leader, she takes her place in the middle of the first row of women and follows the same procedure for the congregational Prayer. The Prophet Muḥammad (PBUH) said that the female servants of Allah should not be prevented from going to the Mosque to pray. All Mosques should therefore, make proper and adequate provisions for women to exercise this right. Women are not obliged to pray in the Mosque as men are, however, and because of their occupation with children may prefer to pray at home.

Women also pray in congregation, either by joining together with the family, neighbourhood or at community level by attending congregational Prayers at the Mosque

Arriving Late for Congregational Prayer

If you arrive to find that the obligatory Prayer has already begun, you should join the row of worshippers and, raising your hands to the level of your ears, palms facing the front, say:

اللهُ أَكْبَر Allāh is Greatest
Allāhu Akbar

then immediately join the worshippers at whatever stage they are at in the Prayer. If it is at the prostration, then go immediately into the prostration position with the rest of the lines. Even if you arrive immediately before the *Imām* is about to conclude the Prayer with the final *Salām*, join the worshippers in their position at that point so that you may get the blessings of Praying in congregation. After the *Imām* has made the final *Salām*, you (without making the *Salām* yourself) should resume your standing position to complete the number of *Rakʿas* you have missed.

If you have joined the Prayer any time up to and including the time of *Rukūʿ*, bowing down (during which the words *Subhana Rabbi al-ʿAẓīm* – 'Glory to Allah the Great' are repeated 3 times), that whole *Rakʿa* is counted.

If you have joined after that time, that is when the *Imām* has resumed the standing position having said *Samiʿa Allāhu liman hamida* – 'Allah hears the one who praises Him', the whole *Rakʿa* and any preceding *Rakʿas* you have missed must be made up.

Attending the Friday or *Jumuʿa* Prayer

Friday Prayer, as it has come to be referred to, or *Jumuʿa* Prayer, takes the place of the noon or *Ẓuhr* Prayer which is normally performed at this time every other day of the week. It consists of two, instead of the normal four *Rakʿas* and is preceded by a sermon or *Khuṭba* which is delivered by the *Imām*.

Friday Prayer, as it has come to be referred to, or *Jumuʿa* Prayer, takes the place of the noon Prayer which is normally performed at this time every other day of the week

The length of the *Khuṭba* will depend on the need and situation. The Prophet Muḥammad (PBUH) recommended that it should be short. It begins after the *Adhān* is called and takes about 20 to 30 minutes. Its purpose is to remind Muslims of the important aspects of Islam in all areas of life and as such can address contemporary social and political issues. It regularly draws the congregation's attention to their relationship with Allah, life after death or the virtues and characteristics of a good Muslim. This is supported by recitation from the Qur'ān and relevant *Ḥadīth*, sayings of the Prophet (PBUH). The *Imām* delivers the *Khuṭba* from the *Minbar*, a pulpit-like structure at the front of the Mosque, during which the worshippers remain in a sitting position neither praying nor talking but listening attentively.

The *Khuṭba* is in two parts: the *Imām*, after delivering the first part in a standing position, sits for a moment before resuming the standing position and commencing with the second part. The second part consists of Praise for Allah, invoking Blessings on the Prophet Muḥammad (PBUH) and the Believers and making supplication for the whole of mankind to establish truth, love, justice, and peace on earth. When the *Imām* has finished the *Khuṭba*, the *Iqāma*, which is the final indication that the Prayer is about to commence, is called. The congregation responds by standing and forming neat and complete rows behind the *Imām* who leads them in the Prayer.

Muslim men are obliged to attend the *Jumuʿa* Prayer in the Mosque or any other venue where it is prayed in congregation. If it is missed, for example, due to:

Muslim men are obliged to attend the *Jumuʿa* Prayer in the Mosque or any other venue where it is Prayed in congregation

- severe weather conditions
- being ill yourself or having to look after someone who is ill
- living or working in a remote area
- if you are travelling
- if you have unsuccessfully tried to negotiate time off work

Jumuʿa Prayer cannot be made up but should be replaced by the original noon, *Ẓuhr* Prayer.

Attendance at *Jumuʿa* Prayer is optional for women who, if not attending, should also replace it with the usual noon, *Ẓuhr* Prayer.

The Festival or *ʿĪd* Prayers

There are two major festivals in Islam. Both commence with a congregational Prayer. One is *ʿĪd al-Fiṭr*, the festival of the breaking of the fast. The other is *ʿĪd al-Aḍḥā*, the festival of sacrifice.

ʿĪd al-Fiṭr falls on the first day of the month of *Shawwāl* following the blessed month of *Ramaḍān* during which the Qur'ān began to be revealed and which is, of course, the month of fasting for every able-bodied Muslim. This festival brings the fasting month to a joyous conclusion.

ʿĪd al-Aḍḥā falls on the tenth day of *Dhū'l-Ḥijja*, the last month of the Muslim calendar, and concludes the *Ḥajj*, the prescribed pilgrimage to Makka. Those who have participated in the *Ḥajj* repent and make the sincere intention to renounce all temptations, renewing their covenant with their Creator to pursue the path of righteousness.

Both of these occasions are celebrated together with the rest of the community. Preparations include cooking special sweetmeats and buying new clothes and gifts for family and friends.

Attending in congregation for the *ʿĪd* Prayer is highly recommended for the whole family. Even women who are having their monthly period, though they are not praying, are strongly recommended to attend with the rest of the family. After the congregational Prayer and in the spirit of

Attending in congregation for the *ʿĪd* Prayer is highly recommended for the whole family. Even women who are having their monthly period, though they are not praying, are strongly recommended to attend with the rest of the family

love and brotherhood, you invite friends and neighbours to celebrate with you in your home.

No *Adhān* or *Iqāma* is required for the *ʿĪd* Prayer which is recited aloud. It consists of 2 *Rakʿas* which commence with the words *Allāhu Akbar* pronounced 7 times at the beginning of the first *Rakʿa* and 5 times preceeding the second *Rakʿa*. After the Prayer is completed the *Imām* delivers a *Khuṭba* to the congregation. On its conclusion the congregation intermingles, wishing each other peace, *Salām* and blessings for the festival of *ʿĪd*.

The Funeral or *Janāza* Prayer

Prayers for the deceased Muslim is a common collective duty on the community. However, if a number of Muslims are present at this time and have attended to this requirement they are representative of the entire community, the rest of whom, though they could not attend, are exempted from the responsibility.

Prayers for the deceased Muslim is a common collective duty on the community. However, if a number of Muslims are present at this time and have attended to this requirement they are representative of the entire community

The *Janāza* or Funeral Prayer is offered in the standing position. The *Imām* stands beside the body and in front of the congregation, all facing in the direction of the *Qibla* and calls *Allāhu Akbar* four times with short intervals between. During these intervals the *Imām* and the congregation recite recommended prayers and supplications silently:

- After the first mention of *Allāhu Akbar* (God is Greatest), *Sūrah al-Fātiḥa* is read.
- After the second, Blessings are invoked on the Prophet Muḥammad (PBUH).
- After the third, a supplication is offered for mercy and forgiveness for the deceased.

- After the fourth and final mention of *Allāhu Akbar*, a supplication is offered for all Muslim men and women, dead and alive.
- The Prayer is concluded as the *Imām*, followed by the congregation, turns his face slightly towards his right shoulder saying *As-Salāmu Alaykum wa Raḥmatullāḥ*. The body is then taken to be buried.

Tarāwīḥ – Night Prayer During the Month of *Ramaḍan*

A special characteristic of *Ramaḍan*, is the *Tarāwīḥ* Prayer. This Prayer may be prayed individually or collectively. It consists of units of 2 *Rakʿas* prayed in pairs similar to the *Fajr* Prayer. It is performed after *ʿIshā'* Prayer and is usually followed by *Shafʿ* and *Witr* Prayers. It is commendable, though not essential, that a reading of the Qur'ān is completed during *Ramaḍan* in the *Tarāwīḥ* Prayer.

Shortening the Prayer

The traveller is given some relief from offering some of the Prayers in their complete form. If one is on a journey, the noon, *Ẓuhr* and afternoon, *ʿAṣr* Prayers are shortened to two *Rakʿas* each. Moreover, permission is also granted for both these shortened Prayers to be Prayed together some time within their given period. To 'Pray them together' means first to Pray the shortened form of one, close with *Salām* as usual and then immediately begin the shortened form of the next Prayer. The evening, *Maghrib* Prayer remains its usual 3 *Rakʿas* but the night, *ʿIshā'* Prayer is reduced to 2 *Rakʿas* with permission also granted to pray both these Prayers together within their given period. The dawn, *Fajr* Prayer remains the same and is prayed at its normal time.

If at any time during your prayer you cannot recall the words, do not lose heart. Simply praise Allah using the simple phrases you may remember

At a Loss for Words

If at any time during your Prayer you cannot recall the words, do not lose heart. Simply praise Allah using the simple phrases you may remember, such as *Allāhu Akbar* – 'Allah is Greatest', or *Subḥan Allāh* – 'Glory to Allah', *Al-Ḥamdulillah* – 'All Praise is due to Allah' and complete the sequence to the end. Time, practice, patience and seeking help from Allah will eventually make you word perfect.

CHAPTER FIVE

MAKING PETITION OR SUPPLICATION – *DUʿĀ'*

Muslims are encouraged to give thanks to Allah for the Bounties He has provided and the Blessings He showers on His servants every day. You are also encouraged to humbly request His help and guidance relating to your everyday problems and concerns. The Prophet (PBUH) encouraged supplication and regarded it as the essence of worship. This can be done in your own words using your mother tongue or in Arabic if you have learned some *Duʿā's*.

When the Prayer is completed, raise your hands and make your petition.

Arabic *du'ā's*

Du'ā' 1

رَبَّنَا *Rabbanā,*	Our Lord,
آتِنَا فِي الدُّنْيَا حَسَنَةً *ātinā fid-dunyā Ḥasanatan*	give us Good in this world
وَفِي الآخِرَةِ حَسَنَةً *wa fil-ākhirati Ḥasanatan*	and Good in the Hereafter,
وَقِنَا عَذَابَ النَّار *wa qinā 'adhāb an-nār*	and save us from the torments of the fire.

Du'ā' 2

رَبِّ اشْرَحْ لِي صَدْرِي *Rabbi ishraḥ lī ṣadrī,*	O my Lord, expand my breast [for understanding/*iman*]
وَيَسِّرْ لِي أَمْرِي *wa yassir lī amrī*	and ease my task for me.

Du'ā' 3

رَبِّ زِدْنِي عِلْماً *Rabbī Zidnī 'ilmā*	O my Lord, advance me in knowledge.

Du'ā' 4

رَبِّ اغْفِرْ وَارْحَمْ *Rabbīghfir warḥam*	O my Lord, grant forgiveness and mercy
وَأَنْتَ خَيْرُ الرَّاحِمِين *wa anta khayrur-rāḥimīn*	for You are the best of those who show mercy.

***Sunna* or Optional Prayers**

Up to now we have dealt only with the compulsory Prayers because they are an obligation on every Muslim, male and female. As you become more confident in both the learning and performance of the Prayer your desire to do more will increase and you will feel compelled to incorporate more of the recommended Prayers, which the Prophet Muḥammad (PBUH) was in the habit of performing and optional Prayers, which you may personally wish to include in your daily routine. They are as follows:

- *Fajr*, Dawn Prayer, **2** highly recommended *Rak'as* before the compulsory Prayer.
- *Ẓuhr*, Noon Prayer, **4** highly recommended *Rak'as* before the compulsory Prayer and **2** highly recommended *Rak'as* after the compulsory Prayer.
- *'Aṣr*, Afternoon Prayer, **4** optional *Rak'as* before the compulsory Prayer.
- *Maghrib*, Sunset Prayer, **2** highly recommended *Rak'as* after the compulsory Prayer.
- *'Ishā'*, Night Prayer, **2** optional *Rak'as* before the compulsory Prayer and **2** after, followed by **1** highly recommended *Rak'a* known as *Witr* or 'odd number'.

These highly recommended and optional Prayers are prayed in addition to the compulsory Prayer and at the same time. In some instances they are prayed prior to, while in others, following the compulsory Prayer.

The *Witr* Prayer is so highly recommended as to be regarded as almost compulsory. It is generally preceded by two *Rakʿas* referred to as *Shafʿ* which literally means 'even number'. These are then followed by one *Rakʿa* of *Witr* which literally means 'odd number'. It is regarded as the final night Prayer and can be prayed anytime during the night after the compulsory *ʿIshāʾ* Prayer (and *Tarāwīḥ* Prayer in *Ramaḍan*) and before *Fajr* Prayer.

CHAPTER SIX

GREETINGS AND OTHER RECOMMENDED EXPRESSIONS

Prayer withdraws you from your routine worldly life for short periods of time and provides an opportunity to remember Allah intensely, with your heart and mind, tongue and limbs. Then, as a Muslim, you must carry out your worldly duties as best you can. The lessons that Prayer imparts, and which should remain with you, are:

(i) Be mindful of Allah; remember that you are always in His Presence and that everything you receive is from Him.
(ii) Remember that everything that happens, happens because He wills it to happen and that nothing you do should violate His teachings.
(iii) Remember Allah as much and as often as you can without giving up or interrupting your normal life.

This remembrance is basically an act of the heart, and though Prayer time allows for this specifically, you are highly encouraged to respond to everything in the form of a Prayer, thus being mindful of Allah at all times. The following are occasions when such responses are recommended:

Think Before You Act

You should commence every action in the name of Allah – eating, drinking, travelling, writing, speaking, etc. Invoking Allah's name makes you more aware that the action you are undertaking is in compliance with His Commands and does not involve something that is wrong or unjust. You should familiarise yourself with this highly recommended habit as you will hear Muslims frequently utter the words:

بِسْمِ اللهِ *Bismillāh*	In the name of Allah

or a longer version

بِسْمِ اللهِ الرَّحْمَنِ الرَّحِيمِ *Bismillāh ir-Raḥmān ir-Raḥim*	In the name of Allah the most Gracious, the most Merciful

Give Praise for Everything

You should be fully conscious of the bounties Allah has set out for all His creation. The belief that He continues to shower His Mercy, Compassion and Blessings on His humble servants expresses itself in words of Praise, whatever the circumstances.

If someone inquires about your health or the well-being of your family, your reply should commence with:

اَلْحَمْدُ لِلّٰهِ *Al-Ḥamdulillāh*	All Praise is to Allah

Greet Each Other Warmly

When Muslims meet they are encouraged to greet each other with blessings invoking peace, and extend hospitality and good-will at home and in the community at large. The Qur'ān reminds us of the following etiquette when greeted:

If you enter houses, salute each other – a greeting of blessing and purity as from Allah. (*Sūrah* 24: 61)

To all those who are God-fearing and believe in the Signs of Creation, the Qur'ān reminds us:

When those come to you who believe in Our Signs say: 'Peace be on you.' (*Sūrah* 6: 54)

You greet another Muslim, therefore, by saying:

السَّلَامُ عَلَيْكُمْ Peace be upon you
As-Salāmu ʿAlaykum

You respond to this greeting with the words:

وَعَلَيْكُمُ السَّلَام And Peace also with you
Wa-ʿAlaykum as-Salām

According to the Qur'ānic verse:

When a courteous greeting is offered to you, meet it with a greeting still more courteous, or at least of equal courtesy. Allah takes full account of all things. (*Sūrah* 4: 86)

Hence you will hear an even longer greeting:

السَّلَامُ عَلَيْكُمْ *As-Salāmu ʿAlaykum*	May the Peace,
وَرَحْمَةُ اللهِ وَبَرَكَاتُه *wa-Raḥmatullāh wa-Barakātuh*	Mercy and Blessings of Allah be with you

You respond with the words:

وَعَلَيْكُمُ السَّلَامُ *Wa ʿAlaykum as-Salām*	And may the Peace,
وَرَحْمَةُ اللهِ وَبَرَكَاتُه *wa-Raḥmatullāh wa-Barakātuh*	Mercy and Blessings of Allah be with you

Give Thanks for Creation

When you experience pleasure, for example, by seeing a new-born baby or feeling awe at the wonders of nature, you are not only moved by the Perfection of Allah's Creation but you should also invoke His Blessings on it by saying:

مَا شَاءَ اللهُ *Māshā' Allah*	Allah has willed it to be so

Purify Your Intention

If you intend to carry out some task in the future or attend to an appointment, be it five minutes, days or years ahead, the expression you use is:

إِنْ شَاءَ اللهُ *Inshā' Allah*	If Allah wills

Remember Allah's Favours

When you encounter an event, a phenomena which is out of the ordinary or you see those less fortunate than yourself, and you are reminded of the favours which Allah has bestowed upon you, you express thanks with the words:

سُبْحَانَ اللهِ *Subḥān Allah*	Glory be to Allah

Pray for the Generous

Receiving and giving gifts is encouraged among Muslims, especially at times of celebration and particularly the two major festivals of *ʿĪd*. When you receive a gift it is preferable, as an expression of thanks, to use a phrases that is a blessing for the giver, such as:

بَارَكَ اللهُ فِيك *Bārakʿallāhu Fīk*	May Allah Bless you

or you may say:

جَزَاكَ اللهُ خَيْراً *Jazākallāhu Khayran*	May Allah Reward you with good

A Sneeze and a Prayer

Muslims are obliged according to the saying of the Prophet (PBUH) to return a blessing on one who sneezes. The one sneezing, should say:

الْحَمْدُ لِلهِ *Al-Ḥamdulillāh*	All Praise is to Allah

You, and anyone who is within earshot, should return the blessing, by saying:

يَرْحَمُكَ اللهُ *Yarḥamuk-Allāh*	May Allah give you Mercy

Remembering Allah in Times of Grief

When you hear of the death of someone or you are suffering some hardship or difficulty, you should say:

إِنَّا لِلهِ وَإِنَّا إِلَيْهِ رَاجِعُون *Innā li-Llāhi wa-innā ilayhi Rājiʿūn*	From Allah we come and to Him is our return

Travel Safely

When you are parting company or going on a journey you may greet others as you would when you meet, using the familiar, *As-Salāmu ʿAlaykum* etc. However there is another very deep and meaningful supplication which you are recommended to extend to the traveller, which is:

فِي أَمَانِ اللهِ *Fī Amānillāh*	May you go with the safety of Allah

Respecting Allah, His Prophets and his Companions

Special attention should be paid when mentioning Allah and His Prophets, particularly the Prophet Muḥammad and his pious Companions both male and female.

When you mention Allah's name it should be followed by the words:

اللهُ سُبْحَانَهُ وَتَعَالَى *Allāh, Subḥānahū wa-Taʿālā*	Allah, Glory be to Him the most High

or

الله عَزَّ وَجَل *Allāh, ʿAzza wa-Jalla*	Allah, the Mighty, the Majestic

When you mention the Prophet Muḥammad's name it should be followed by the words:

مُحَمَّدٌ صَلَّى اللهُ عَلَيهِ وَسَلَّمْ *Muḥammad, Ṣallallāhu ʿAlayhi wa Salam*	Muḥammad, May the Peace and Blessings of Allah be upon him

If you mention any of the Prophets other than Muḥammad (PBUH), this is followed by the words:

مُوسَى عَلَيْهِ السَّلاَم *Mūsā, ʿAlayhis-Salām*	Moses, Peace be upon him
عِيسَى عَلَيْهِ السَّلاَم *ʿĪsa, ʿAlayhis-Salām*	Jesus, Peace be upon him

Male Companions of the Prophet (PBUH) are mentioned thus:

أَبُوبَكْر رَضِيَ الله عَنْه *Abū Bakr, Raḍiya-Allāhu ʿanhu*	Abu Bakr, may Allah be pleased with him

Female Companions of the Prophet (PBUH) are mentioned thus:

خَدِيجَة رَضِيَ الله عَنْهَا *Khadīja, Raḍiya-Allāhu ʿanhā*	Khadīja, may Allah be pleased with her

Allah's Mercy and Forgiveness is Endless

When you hear or see anything bad or immoral or fear you have done something incorrect you should immediately turn to Allah for forgiveness. In this event you should say:

أَسْتَغْفِرُ اللّٰه *Astaghfirullāh*	I seek forgiveness from Allah

CHAPTER SEVEN

THE PERFORMANCE OF THE DAWN OR FAJR PRAYER IN ARABIC

(WITH ILLUSTRATIONS)

Step 1. Standing on clean ground, mat or clean cover you begin by making the intention, *Niyya*, to pray this *Fajr* Prayer for the sake of Allah.
Then raising your hands to the level of your ears, with palms facing the front, say:

Allāhu Akbar

Step 2.

Lower your arms to the centre of your body, the right hand resting on the left hand, and recite the opening *Sūrah* of the Qur'ān, *Sūrah al-Fātiḥa*:

Bismillāh ir-Raḥmān ir-Raḥim
Al-Ḥamdu lillāhi rabbi-l-ʿĀlamīn
Ar-Raḥmān ir-Raḥīm
Māliki yawmid-dīn
Iyyāka naʿbudu wa iyyāka nastaʿīn
Ihdinaṣ-ṣirāṭal-mustaqīm
ṣirāṭal-ladhīna an ʿamta ʿalayhim
ghayri-l-maghḍūbi ʿalayhim walāḍ-ḍālīn
Āmīn

(This is followed with another short *Sūrah* from the Qur'ān which you are recommended to learn and recite when you can. This applies to the first two *Rakʿas* of the Prayer only.)

Step 3.

After this you say: *Allāhu Akbar*

Now bow, with your hands gripping your knees and your back and head level, and repeat three times:

Subḥāna Rabbī al-ʿAẓim

Step 4.
Resuming the upright position with your hands by your sides, say:

Samiʿa Allāhu liman ḥamida
Rabbanā walakal-ḥamd

Step 5.
Repeat the words:
Allāhu Akbar

From the standing position lower yourself to a kneeling position, your forehead and nose touching the ground, the palms of your hands flat on the ground each side of your head. Your arms and elbows should not touch the floor. You are now in the prostration position. In this position say, 3 times:

Subḥāna Rabbi al-ʿAla

Step 6.

Repeat the words: *Allāhu Akbar*

Then sit back on your feet with your hands resting on your thighs near to your knees. In this position it is highly recommended to supplicate and ask Allah for forgiveness and Mercy.

Step 7.

After a moment or two, repeat: *Allāhu Akbar*

Return to the prostration position, repeating as before 3 times:

Subḥāna Rabbi al-Aʿla

This completes one *Rakʿa* of the Prayer.

To carry on with the second *Rakʿa*, stand and repeat the words *Allāhu Akbar* followed by Steps 2-7.

Step 8.
To conclude the prescribed two *Rakʿas* of the Dawn or *Fajr* Prayer, repeat: *Allāhu Akbar*

Sitting back on your feet and resting your hands on your thighs near to your knees, similar to the position you assumed between the two prostrations, you raise your right index finger and recite the following prayer known as the *Tashahhud*:

At-Taḥiyyātu Lillāhi
Waṣ-Ṣalawātu Waṭ-Ṭayyibātu
As-salāmu ʿAlayka Ayyuhan-Nabiyyu
Wa Raḥmatullāhi Wa Barakātuhu
As-Salāmu ʿAlaynā
wa ʿAlā Ibādillāhiṣ-Ṣaliḥīn

Ashadu an lā ilāha illāllāh
Wa-ashhadu anna Muḥammadan
ʿAbduhū wa Rasūluh

(This is followed by the prayer known as *aṣ-Ṣalat ʿalā an-Nabī* or prayer on the Prophet (PBUH) which, though it is not required to complete your Prayer, you should learn and recite as soon as you can).

Allāhumma ṣalli ʿalā Muḥammad
wa ʿalā āli Muḥammad
kamā ṣallayta ʿalā Ibrāhīm
wa ʿalā āli Ibrāhīm
innaka ḥamīdun majīd
Allāhumma Bārik ʿalā Muḥammad

wa ʿalā āli Muḥammad
kamā bārakta ʿalā Ibrāhīm
wa ʿalā āli Ibrāhīm
innaka ḥamīdun majīd

Step 9.
Finally, turn your head and looking towards your right shoulder, say: *As-Salāmu ʿAlaykum wa Raḥmatullāh* – and turning to your left and looking towards your left shoulder, say: *As-Salāmu ʿAlaykum wa Raḥmatullāh*.

This final *Salām* completes the requirements for the dawn or *Fajr* Prayer. The same instructions apply to the *Ẓuhr*, *ʿAṣr* or *ʿIsha'* Prayers when they are shortened (see p. 45).

If you are performing one of the other four daily Prayers which necessitate one or two more *Rakʿas*, you simply recite the *Tashahhud* after the first two *Rakʿas*, then resume the standing position repeating the words *Allāhu Akbar* and complete one or two more *Rakʿas*, according to the Prayer in question and end with the *Tashahhud* (and *aṣ Ṣalat 'alā an-Nabī* when you are able) and make the final *Salām*. In the third and fourth *Rakʿas* of a Prayer, you should recite *Sūrah al-Fātiḥa* only.

APPENDIX

Short *Sūrahs* from the Qur'ān

Chapter 106. **The Tribe of Quraysh**

بِسْمِ اللهِ الرَّحْمَٰنِ الرَّحِيمِ *Bismillāh ir-Raḥmān ir-Raḥīm*	In the name of Allah, the Most Gracious the Most Merciful
لِإِيلَٰفِ قُرَيْشٍ *Li'ilāfi Quraysh*	For the benefit of the Quraysh;
إِۦلَٰفِهِمْ رِحْلَةَ ٱلشِّتَآءِ وَٱلصَّيْفِ *Ilāfihim riḥlatash-shitāi waṣ-ṣayf*	for their benefit the caravans go out in the winter and summer
فَلْيَعْبُدُوا۟ رَبَّ هَٰذَا ٱلْبَيْتِ *Falyaʿbudū Rabba hadhā al-bayt*	So they should worship the Lord and Sustainer of this House, (the Kaʿbah)
ٱلَّذِىٓ أَطْعَمَهُم مِّن جُوعٍ وَءَامَنَهُم مِّنْ خَوْفٍۭ *Al-ladhī' aṭʿamahum min jūʿin wa āmanahum min khawf*	Who has fed them, protected them from hunger, and made them safe from fear.

Chapter 107. **Simple Acts of Kindness (*Al-Māʿūn*)**

بِسْمِ اللهِ الرَّحْمَنِ الرَّحِيمِ *Bismillāh ir-Raḥmān ir-Raḥīm*	In the name of Allah, the Most Gracious the Most Merciful
أَرَءَيْتَ ٱلَّذِى يُكَذِّبُ بِٱلدِّينِ *Ara'ayta al-ladhī yukad-dhibu bid-dīn*	Have you seen the one who denies religion?
فَذَٰلِكَ ٱلَّذِى يَدُعُّ ٱلْيَتِيمَ *Fadhālika al-ladhī yaduʿu al-yatīm*	– the one who pushes the orphan aside,
وَلَا يَحُضُّ عَلَىٰ طَعَامِ ٱلْمِسْكِينِ *Wa-lā yaḥuḍḍu ʿalā taʿamil-miskīn*	and does not encourage feeding the poor people?
فَوَيْلٌ لِّلْمُصَلِّينَ *Fa-waylun lil-muṣallīn*	Oh, wretched are the worshippers
ٱلَّذِينَ هُمْ عَن صَلَاتِهِمْ سَاهُونَ *Al-ladhīna hum ʿan Ṣalātihim sāhūn*	who are negligent in their Prayers!
ٱلَّذِينَ هُمْ يُرَآءُونَ *Al-ladhīna hum yurā-ūn*	The ones who show off (in Prayer)
وَيَمْنَعُونَ ٱلْمَاعُونَ *Wa-yamnaʿuna al-māʿūn*	but refuse simple acts of kindness!

Chapter 108. **Abundance (of all that is good) (*Al-Kawthar*)**

بِسْمِ اللهِ الرَّحْمَنِ الرَّحِيمِ
Bismillāh ir-Raḥmān ir-Raḥīm

In the name of Allah, the Most Gracious the Most Merciful

إِنَّآ أَعْطَيْنَـٰكَ ٱلْكَوْثَرَ
Innā a'taynāka al-kawthar

Surely We have given you the fountain of Abundance

فَصَلِّ لِرَبِّكَ وَٱنْحَرْ
Fa-ṣalli lirabbika wanḥar

so Pray to your Lord, and make sacrifice.

إِنَّ شَانِئَكَ هُوَ ٱلْأَبْتَرُ
Inna shāni'aka huwal-abtar

Surely it is the one who insults you [Muḥammad, and not you] who will leave no one behind to remember him.

Chapter 109. **The Unbelievers (*Al-Kāfirūn*)**

بِسْمِ اللهِ الرَّحْمَنِ الرَّحِيمِ
Bismillāh ir-Raḥmān ir-Raḥīm

In the name of Allah, the Most Gracious the Most Merciful

قُلْ يَـٰٓأَيُّهَا ٱلْكَـٰفِرُونَ
Qul yā-ayyuh'al-kāfirūn

Say: 'O, unbelievers!'

لَآ أَعْبُدُ مَا تَعْبُدُونَ
lā aʿbudu mā taʿbudūn

I do not worship what you worship,

وَلَآ أَنتُمْ عَـٰبِدُونَ مَآ أَعْبُدُ
wa-lā antum ʿabiduna mā aʿbud

and you do not worship what I worship.

وَلَآ أَنَا۠ عَابِدٌ مَّا عَبَدتُّمْ
Wa-lā ana ʿabidun mā ʿabadtum

and I will not worship what you worship,

وَلَآ أَنتُمْ عَـٰبِدُونَ مَآ أَعْبُدُ
Wa-lā antum ʿabiduna mā-aʿbud

and you do not worship what I worship,

لَكُمْ دِينُكُمْ وَلِىَ دِينِ
Lakum dīnukum waliya dīn

(So,) for you is your way, and for me is mine.'

Chapter 110. **The Help (*Al-Naṣr*)**

بِسْمِ اللهِ الرَّحْمَنِ الرَّحِيمِ
Bismillāh ir-Raḥmān ir-Raḥīm

In the name of Allah, the Most Gracious the Most Merciful

إِذَا جَآءَ نَصْرُ ٱللَّهِ وَٱلْفَتْحُ
ʿĪdha jā'a naṣrullāhi wal-fatḥ

When Allah's help comes, and a successful victory,

وَرَأَيْتَ ٱلنَّاسَ يَدْخُلُونَ فِى دِينِ ٱللَّهِ أَفْوَاجًا
wa-ra' aytan-nāsa yadkhulūna fī-dīnillāhi afwājā

and you see people accepting Allah's religion in masses,

فَسَبِّحْ بِحَمْدِ رَبِّكَ وَٱسْتَغْفِرْهُ
fasabbiḥ biḥamdi rabbika wastaghfirh

then remember to praise your Lord and ask Him for forgiveness.

إِنَّهُۥ كَانَ تَوَّابَۢا *innahu kāna tawwābā*	Surely He is always ready to forgive.

Chapter 111. **The Flame/The Palm Leaf (*Al-Lahab/Al-Masad*)**

بِسْمِ اللهِ الرَّحْمَٰنِ الرَّحِيمِ *Bismillāh ir-Raḥmān ir-Raḥīm*	In the name of Allah, the Most Gracious the Most Merciful
تَبَّتْ يَدَآ أَبِي لَهَبٍ وَتَبَّ *Tabbat yada Abi lahabin wa-tabb*	The power of Abu Lahab will perish, and he will perish
مَآ أَغْنَىٰ عَنْهُ مَالُهُۥ وَمَا كَسَبَ *Ma-aghna anhu maluhu wa-ma kasab*	Neither his wealth nor what he has gained will help him
سَيَصْلَىٰ نَارًا ذَاتَ لَهَبٍ *Sayaslā naran dhata lahab*	He will be pushed down into the flaming Fire
وَٱمْرَأَتُهُۥ حَمَّالَةَ ٱلْحَطَبِ *Wamraatuhu hammalata al-hatab*	and his wife, the wood-carrier
فِي جِيدِهَا حَبْلٌ مِّن مَّسَدٍۭ *Fi-jidiha hablun min masad*	will have a rope of rough palm leaves around her neck.

Chapter (112). **The Purity or Sincerity of Faith (*Al-Ikhlas*)**

بِسْمِ اللهِ الرَّحْمَنِ الرَّحِيمِ *Bismillāh ir-Raḥmān ir-Raḥīm*	In the name of Allah, the Most Gracious the Most Merciful
قُلْ هُوَ ٱللَّهُ أَحَدٌ *Qul huwa Allāhu ahad*	Say: 'He is Allah the one and only
ٱللَّهُ ٱلصَّمَدُ *Allāhus-samad*	Allah the Eternal, Absolute
لَمْ يَلِدْ وَلَمْ يُولَدْ *Lam yalid wa-lam yulad*	He does not give birth and He was not born
وَلَمْ يَكُن لَّهُۥ كُفُوًا أَحَدٌۢ *wa-lam yakun lahu kufuwan ahad*	and there is nothing (at all) like Him.'

Chapter (113). **The Dawn (*Al-Falaq*)**

بِسْمِ اللهِ الرَّحْمَنِ الرَّحِيمِ *Bismillāh ir-Raḥmān ir-Raḥīm*	In the name of Allah, the Most Gracious the Most Merciful
قُلْ أَعُوذُ بِرَبِّ ٱلْفَلَقِ *Qul aʿūdhu bi-rabbil-falaq*	Say: 'I seek safety and protection in the Lord of the dawn
مِن شَرِّ مَا خَلَقَ *Min sharri mā-khalaq*	from the evil of the things He created,

وَمِن شَرِّ غَاسِقٍ إِذَا وَقَبَ *Wa-min sharri ghāsī'qin idhā waqab*	from the evil of the darkness when it is very strong
وَمِن شَرِّ ٱلنَّفَّـٰثَـٰتِ فِى ٱلْعُقَدِ *Wa-min sharrin-naffāthāti fi'l-ʿuqad*	from the evil of people who practise witchcraft,
وَمِن شَرِّ حَاسِدٍ إِذَا حَسَدَ *Wa-min sharri ḥāsidin idhā ḥasad*	and from the evil of the envious one when he envies'.

Chapter (114). **The people (*An-Nas*)**

بِسْمِ اللهِ الرَّحْمَنِ الرَّحِيم *Bismillāh ir-Raḥmān ir-Raḥīm*	In the name of Allah, the Most Gracious the Most Merciful
قُلْ أَعُوذُ بِرَبِّ ٱلنَّاسِ *Qul aʿūdhu bi-Rabbin-nās*	Say: 'I seek refuge and protection in the Lord of all people,
مَلِكِ ٱلنَّاسِ *Malikin-nās*	the King of all people,
إِلَـٰهِ ٱلنَّاسِ *Ilāhin-nās*	the God of all people,
مِن شَرِّ ٱلْوَسْوَاسِ ٱلْخَنَّاسِ *Min sharril-waswāsil-khannās*	from the evil of those who whisper secretly,

ٱلَّذِى يُوَسْوِسُ فِى صُدُورِ ٱلنَّاسِ
Al-ladhī yuwaswisu fī ṣudurin-nās

who whisper (evil) into the hearts of people

مِنَ ٱلْجِنَّةِ وَٱلنَّاسِ
Min al-jinnati wan-nās

from (those evil ones of) the *jinn* and the people.'

The New Muslims Project

Bringing New Muslims Together

The New Muslims Project welcomes those new to or interested in Islam, offering a wide range of friendly and accessible services:

Meeting Point
a free quarterly newsletter.

Pilgrimage
facilitating Hajj and Umrah for those new to Islam.

A Simple Guide to Prayer
a book with accompanying CD.

Qur'anic Arabic Courses
week long residential courses.

National Network
trained volunteers offer individual local support.

Advice and Counselling
support through the transition of conversion.

eGroup
a discussion forum where issues are explored.

NMP Website
encourages learning and instruction on aspects of Islam.

Shahadah Certificates
useful documentation for marriage, travel, and Hajj.

Gift Packs
a gift pack as a memento of converting to Islam.

Ramadan Retreats
an opportunity to pray and break fast together.

Eid Open Days
celebrating Eid with family and friends.

and lots more besides...

For further information and advice
please contact:
New Muslims Project,
The Islamic Foundation,
Ratby Lane, Markfield,
Leicestershire, LE67 9SY.
Tel: 01530 244937
Fax: 01530 244946
E-mail:
batool@islamic-foundation.org.uk
Website:
www.newmuslimsproject.net

NOTES